"Always stay on the bridge between the invisible and the visible."

**Paulo Coelho**

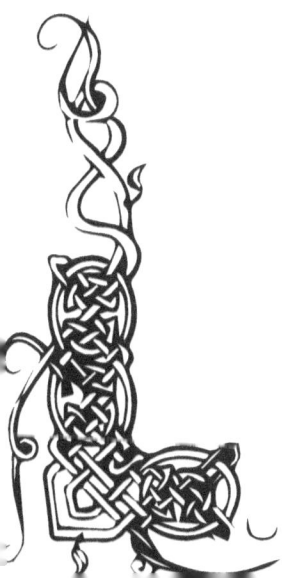

# Grimoire

by Jacob R. Moses

iiPUBLISHING

# Grimoire

Copyright © 2021 by Jacob R. Moses

## Poems previously published in Magazines:

"Bestiary" (Synkroniciti, 2021)*
"Willow in the Wind" (Dreams Walking, 2020)*
"Lingua Franca" (Verse-Virtual, 2020)*
"When You Can't Dream" (NYPL St. George Library, 2020)*
"The Auroras & Blossoms NaPoWriMo Anthology" (Auroras & Blossoms, 2020)*
"Survivor" (Unspoken Word, 2020)*
"The Revolution" (Verse-Virtual, 2020)*
"Essential" (Verse-Virtual, 2020)*
"Celestial Mirror" (E-Shalom, 2020)*
"Autumn Leaves" (OpenDoor Poetry Magazine, 2020)
"Through the Branches" (OpenDoor Poetry Magazine, 2020)
"Spike" (OpenDoor Poetry Magazine, 2020)

*Published under the alias Jack M. Freedman*

Cover design & illustrations by tonii

ISBN: 979-8-9850204-0-3

Printed in the United States of America

## iiPUBLISHING

ancestors

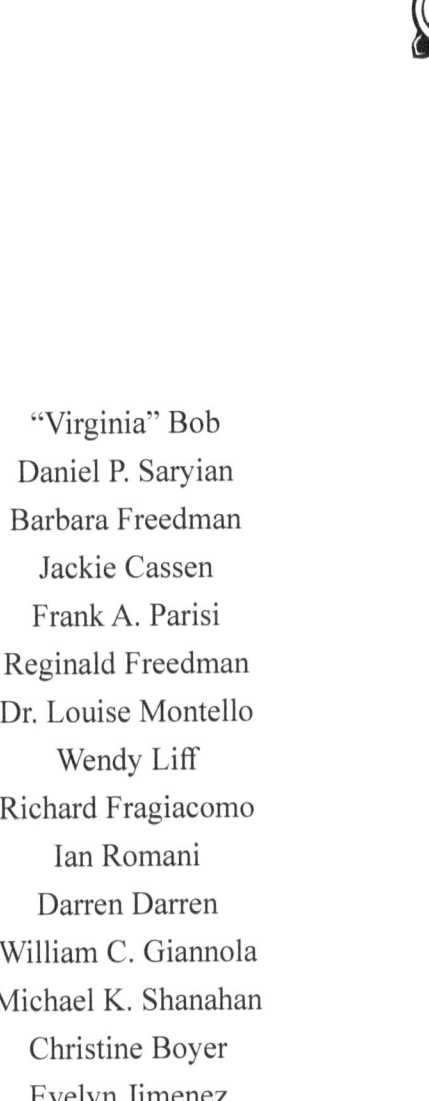

"Virginia" Bob
Daniel P. Saryian
Barbara Freedman
Jackie Cassen
Frank A. Parisi
Reginald Freedman
Dr. Louise Montello
Wendy Liff
Richard Fragiacomo
Ian Romani
Darren Darren
William C. Giannola
Michael K. Shanahan
Christine Boyer
Evelyn Jimenez
Leigh A. Perry

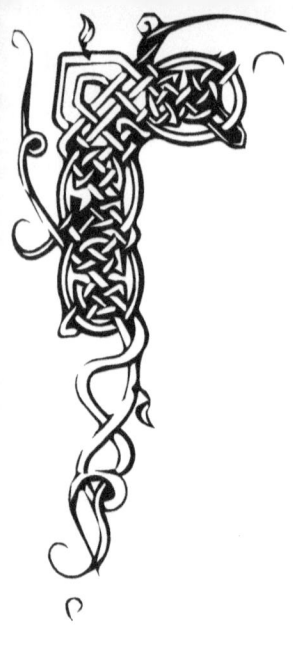

# contents

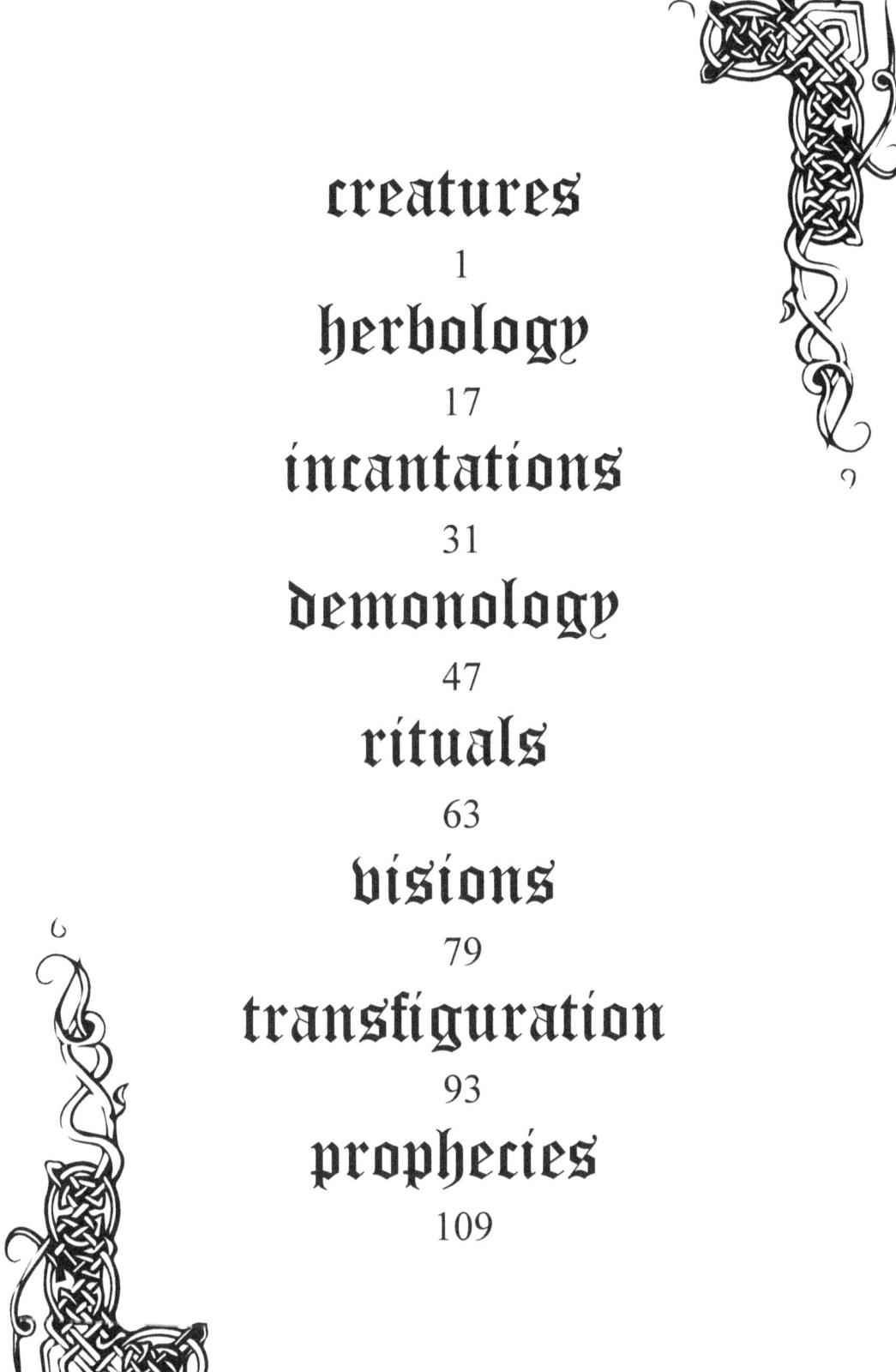

# invocation

As I started writing Grimoire, I realized this was going to be a project in which many of my defenses would be dropped. Choices and decisions were rooted in demons I attempted to exorcise. They took the form of battling the depression which came from addiction, grief, and isolation. I needed to relearn that which used to come easy. Tasks as simple as waking up, showering, and eating were not second nature anymore. Sometimes, writing could be included as an unchecked item on my to-do list. However, it was my newfound spirituality which allowed me to find different muses. Some of which were the nine muses in Greek mythology and others were the very pain I experienced in the process of repairing myself. Grimoire was the sunshine I needed to illuminate a damaged sense of self.

At certain points, April was a month of alchemical transmutation. In the tradition of National Poetry Writing Month, I attempted to write thirty poems within the span of thirty days. Four of the years I attempted this feat proved to be successful. The true paydirt came from knowing that I was capable of releasing such immense bursts of creativity. I figured that if I was able to work through years of mental health issues, I could turn my pain into gold. Moreover, I could unearth the abundance I'd been trying to unearth throughout my forty years on this planet. Nearly half of those years were spent perfecting my craft as a poet. Many of them were spent perfecting the performance elements of poetry. Others were spent submitting those same poems to numerous publications around the world.

In the occult, a grimoire is a book in which those who practice magick log their spells. During my time as a wizard, I kept a number of journals in which I'd recorded the depths of my mystical and spiritual journeys. During these voyages, I had a number of deaths within my burdensome and paralyzing thoughts. It would only be at those points where I would find gold. Wizardry allowed me to truly envision how to embrace the light and balance it with the pre-existing darkness I faced during debilitating bouts of depression. It also allowed me to embrace my role as a guardian. As I write this invocation, my son Owen is starting his freshman year of college. It is gratifying to know that his magick lies within his visual art.

In the two decades that I've been a poet, I've kept the wheels of my creativity moving. My writing got me through periods where I felt generational curses would be a mainstay. Grimoire is a collection of forty years of wisdom I developed through braving the earthquakes, infernos, hurricanes, and tsunamis in my life. Bitter as I became during many of those extraordinary circumstances I experienced with bipolar mixed states, I found sweetness. I realized that there was a philosopher's stone I could use to transmute my fragile state of mind, heart, body, and spirit. A healthy awareness of my struggles would lead me to find the treasure within myself. My sense of glory came strictly from surviving my greatest fears. I wish for the same self-discovery to all who read my work. There is more than one way to unlock potential and find the magick within.

My name is Jacob R. Moses.
I am the Wizard of Willow.
This is Grimoire.

# grimoire

[grim'wär]

*a book of magic spells and invocations.*

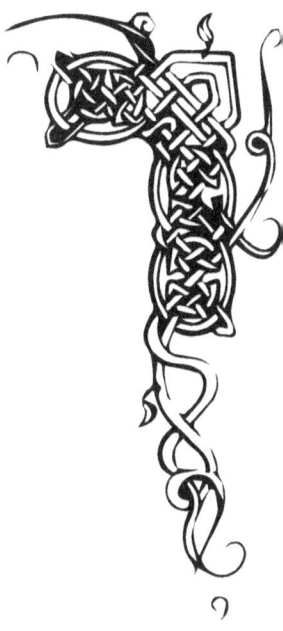

# creatures

represents the beasts which lie within the human soul. Within this set of poems is the sanctuary of animal instincts. Each of these poems are clues to discovering the beast within.

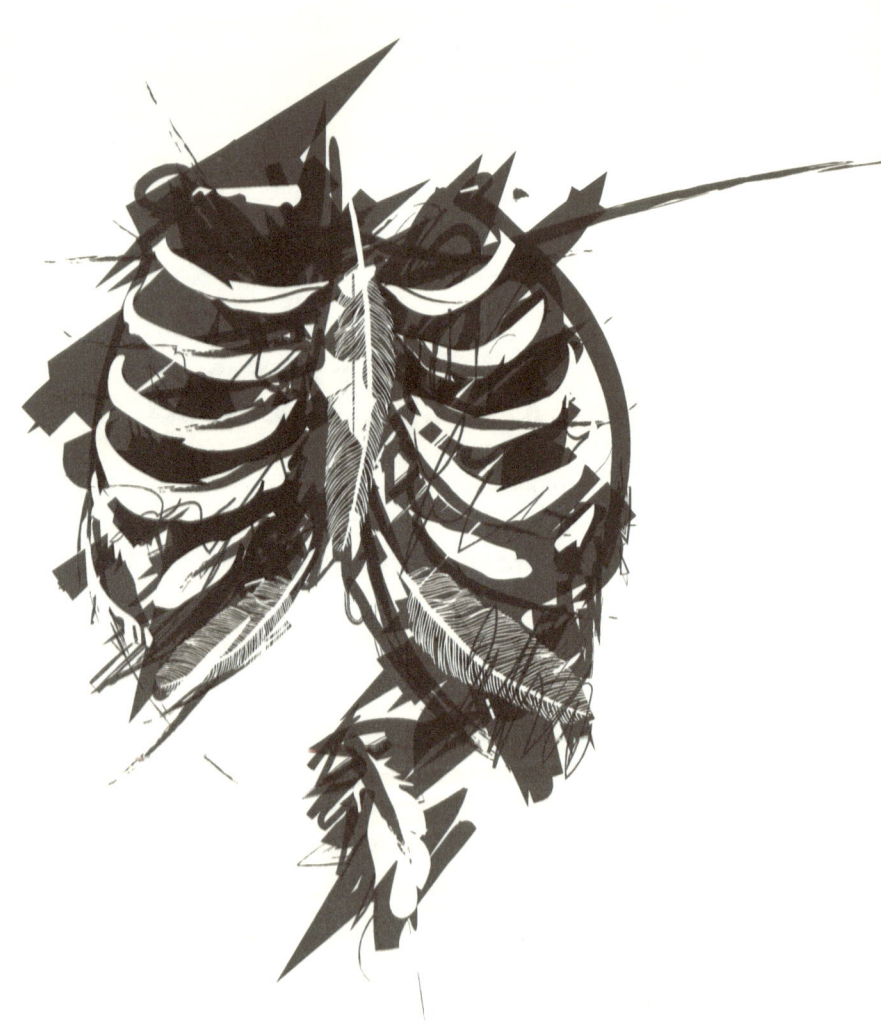

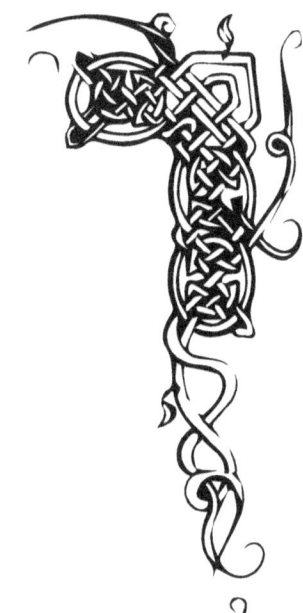

Crows, black with intensity
Doves, white with my empathy
Pelicans have gelled with me
Phoenix filled with entropy
Peacock melds the alchemy
Owls emit the head of me
Falcons see the hell I see
Pink flamingos, heavenly
Swans, the elegance of glee
Seagulls are my destiny
Robins, red like my belly
Eagles on my wounded knee.

Ova

As I spit my gospels
my tongue is forked
and tuned at a high pitch

I sing arias of acerbic aridity
salty and dry are my octaves

This earth upon which I crawl
is polluted with human waste.
I shed the skin off my snaky squalor.
Segments of my scales are sliced.

Could you get close to me?
Could you allow my passion to constrict you?

My body aches,
withered by thorns and glass

But I continue singing.
My hissed hymns

wrap around kissed limbs
I crawl on my belly
Sometimes finding refuge
in the sea
My shanties are those of vengeance
against human tyranny

I wake up
the glass upon which I crawled
was one I broke
Amid a high pitched scream,
carried by rage.

Feeling the condemnation of God
for the origin of my sins.

### Serpentine Soprano

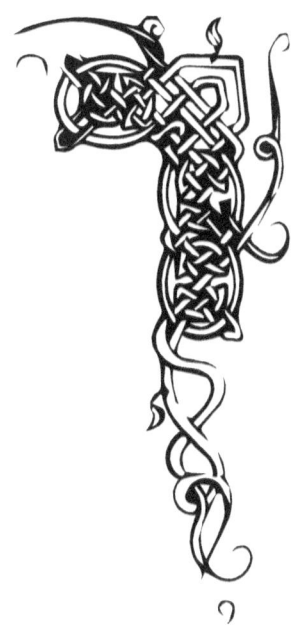

Amethyst camel
Crested in the finest gold
Leads the caravan
Mother's spirit animal
Infused with father's birthstone.

Amethyst Camel

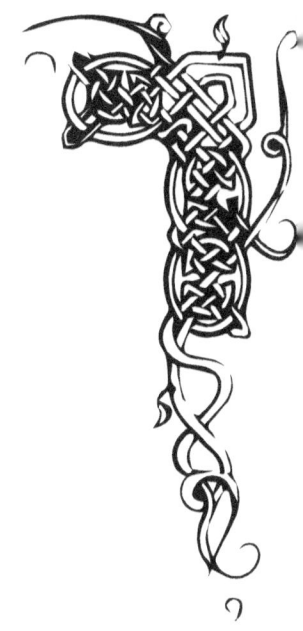

r obins
spring birth
messenger of peace
birds bridge many realms
from the departed
sent through
crows.

Diamanté: Robins + Crows

From sound frequencies
blaring through light
creatures roam the terrains
of my subconscious

With a ballpoint
I am the vessel
in which my wildfire
initiates the genesis
of a new world
within a leather bound
graveyard of trees

Images of these beasts
assert dominance
over my non-dominant hand

Intuition guides me to identify
the taxonomy of
my broken sense of clarity

Only to be classified as
a recluse with imaginary friends
in images which would be
unrecognizable to those
far less magical and
significantly less imaginative

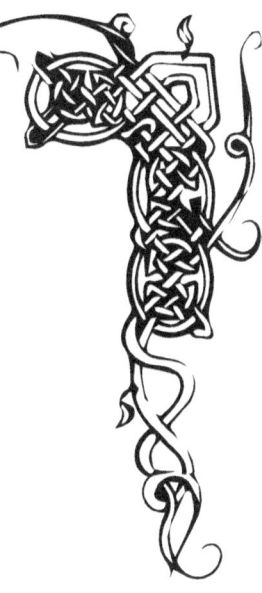

These are transmissions
which are sent through me
with the reserved fervor
initiated by the sounds of
Egypt and Tibet

I am the conjurer
who walks a fine line in this
alley of grayness

I am the beast
taking the form of animals
which have long been symbols
of my spiritual DNA

In the truest of forms
this bestiary holds
the broken

And these pages
are the glue

These are the clues
to help me sleuth
how I may be whole
once again.

Bestiary

My moods are vines
upon which baboons
sweep the shady side
of willows.

Answer this call.
This primal release
of nobility
bounces and ricochets
within weathered walls.

I plummeted into a
pit of hyenas,
fate predetermined
fall of fraternity
abdication
of Honor's throne.

I lead the pride

amid the falsehood,

not too proud
to combat the
phoniness.
My heart bruised
by belligerence.

Know me
as one who
possesses love
amid the lesions

My eyes are bloodshot,
smoke born from the friction
between me and the world.

But nonetheless
clarity remains

Leo Rising

All shall hail King Darius in a white cage
Never saw the creation of a palace
Lived inside a bachelor pad of a birdcage
Blue and white martyr

O' Queen Jane, albino, white feathers, red eyes
She most likely overthrowing King Darius
On one summer day, he wound up flat lining
She was the culprit

Kofi - green and yellow bird was the next one
Womanizer, fought with Queen Jane immensely
Met a bad demise as one of four budgies
Must have been hen pecked

We must never forget about King Saffron
Father of three chicks and he is still reigning
Yellow feathers, green and black accents, boldness
Dedicated dad

Frost - the matriarch of the tallest mansion
Lost one chick, she laid five more eggs, maternal
Three hatched, lovely indigo feathers, soulful
Death by egg binding

Green-yellow, Safari was once a free range
Took up residence in my mother's chamber
Lost Queen Jane, loved her with undying passion
Local adventures

Amazon - the white bird donned in confetti
Keeps to himself - chronically transcendental
Roommate with Safari - it seems to have worked
Now they are buddies

Koa - first born, yellow with wingtips blackened
Pride of Frost and King Saffron, birthright offered
Sits on swings and rocks, overlooking the sun
Heart of Hawaii

Epic now is Erica, yellow also
Speckled with gray feathers, poised like a leopard
Now Safari's main squeeze, he dances for her
Eyes of affection

Last born Sigil - Frost and King Saffron's baby
Faintly silver accents adorn bright yellow
Quiet - but observant from every view of
Her tail's flirtations.

**Parakeet Song**

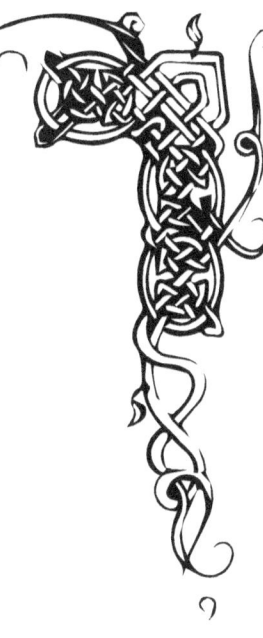

Multitude of earth
dwelling nocturnal
creatures, blissful

in the links between
shadows and ecstasy
Into this moon, stare

deep into the heaven
in between clouds, on
top of quasars, burst

of the nebulous, rain
distantly reflects
desires of id, libido

quenched by red wine
Dance of midnight, an
aphorism, primal ego,

unpredictable yaw, a
shift of levity, moor
where roses fly east

Retrograde orbit, we
will undo these wars
Reneged prophecies

Apocalyptic refund
Golden ratio intact
Aesthetically pure

is this celebration
Collective indigo
intuits connection

## Land of the Night

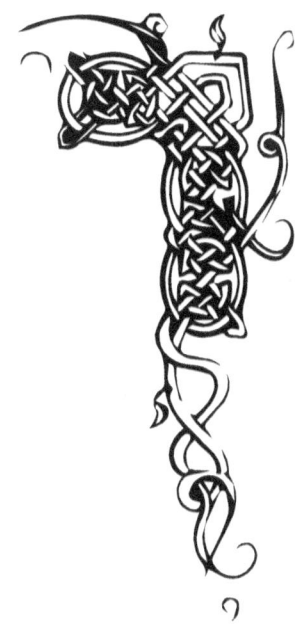

# herbology

*represents the love of flora. The connection to plant life is a
powerful one. We share a symbiotic relationship with them
and it's best to leave yourself open to synchronicity.*

You watched me fall apart,
sweeping the petals of my security
into the gutter of your disdain

Once again,
stripped of love
By the wayside
falls the bevy of rose petals
surrounding my feet
numb from diabetes and dichotomies

Your eyes will perceive me
as either yin or yang,
one or the other.
Never both.
You neglect the trouble and triumph
within my swirls.

I scale, I rappel, I scale, I rappel, I scale, I rappel

Praying I don't collapse
If I fall,
I would rather glide
like my petals from days of yore.

I hope one day,
one may love me unconditionally
instead of plucking away at me
relying on superstition over reason.
Nourish me with acceptance.

I love you...
I love you not...
I love you...
I love you not...
I love you...
I love you not...
I love...

**Urban Bloom**

W ind comforts my soul and as sure as
I am the weeping tree which will simply
Laugh with the breezes
Lay in the soil
My branches will not
Only sway near the grass
But I always wave
Without the threat
Of a clean break.

## Willow in the Wind

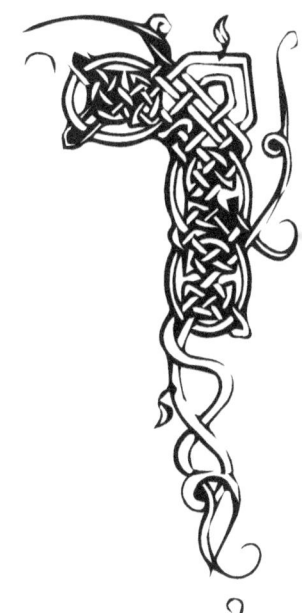

$\mathfrak{E}$levation of these vines soothe
My wrathful state of grapes.
Born to enter a mirthful
Rite of passage the fruit must embody.
Youthful are the seeds in the
Ovaries of Mother
Nature as she hums harmonically
In synchrony with the bees,
Collectively pollinating a new life.
Askew is the alignment as the
Latitudes are crossed and the
Longitudes are exceeded.
Yards of vines shape this garden.

### Birth of a Vineyard

$\mathfrak{F}$ ire falls and frost flourishes
Autumn is alive as leaves die

The heart remains evergreen
when color disperses through
its network of vessels

Every breeze is a reminder of mortality
and every fabric which protects
ultimately shields

Release the aura
before winter's arrival
letting laurels lie
allow cosmic migration
to fill spaces

prevalence
of yin and yang dwells
within sky and ground

## Seasonal Hybrid

Would you care to jump
in a pile of autumn leaves
under this white birch?

Come snap a photo
of your exploits as you dive
into this foliage.

In sweater weather,
you can feel the crunchiness
in your wind-chapped palms.

Stripping this bark bare,
you can feel the heat as you
find a branch to climb.

You need only one
source of vegetation where
these twigs emanate.

Now you may join me
as the brisk wind embraces
and the sap pours out.

## Autumn Leaves

Celestial and surreal
Leaves loosely
Blanket the sunset

Where the horizon meets
Crickets sing the coming
Of crimson descent

Reminiscent of the sea
Forming a gradient meld
With Bermudian sand

Branches mimic the curtains
Yet still reveal the essence
Of a heaven embodying stillness

But a colder equinox makes way
As air accelerates
Breezing between bark

Never forget the roots
These images remind us of
Ancestry neglected

Loosening of dogma
Abandonment of shame
Serenity within illumination.

## Through the Branches

No magma exists within me,
but I am adorned by lava.
It drips from my pores,
scorching the earth around me.

No solid ground to stand upon.
I am a mountain of molten madness.

I am a foundation
suspended only by fire,
leaves erupt from within this mass.
They are fertile from photosynthesis,
green, fragrant, highness imbued within the facade.

This flame will arouse you.
This flame will ignite conversations.
This flame will spark the leaves
which release pheromones
lacking when improvement

sizzles and shrivels

like bacon on the back burner.
I embrace my fiery exterior.
I wish not
to stay dormant
for decades.

I hold out for hope
that the beacon of herbal eruption
is laced within a landscape
which gives me the rocks
I need to suspend myself.

As a volcano,
I am solid within my solitude.
I have my pathways to a gentle nature.
Leaves link like ladders
forming gardens which emanate from my private Babylon.
I will stay strong.
I will hang on.

# Herbal Eruption

My only riches stem
from that which decomposes

Mushrooms are markers
Monoliths of the morbid

Derived from
the bowels of the social food chain

Bury my past
I will emerge
as my redness expands
above my shoulders

My waist weighs
within this waste

One kiss
exposes you to possibilities
of color

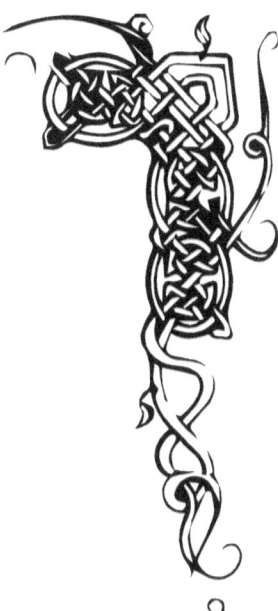

expanded beyond
ten dozen
cylinders of wax
wrapped in paper
sheathed in cardboard

Forgive my past
Taste the present
Ponder our future

The overlooked
need more
attention
I am no exception

I refuse
to let my beauty
remain
neglected.

The Road to Muscaria

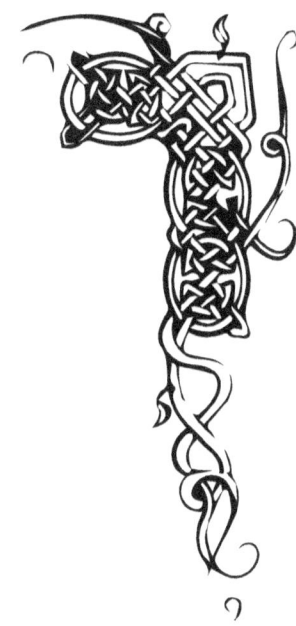

# incantations

*represents intentions put into the universe. Whether these verses rhyme or have affirmations, they are a key to a portal of poetry. Rest assured, you will not turn into a frog or bat while reading this section.*

Geometry within a sacred shrine
No conquest of this village can degrade
Illuminated staircase, bright moonshine
Our apparitions emanate from shade
Tall gates extending for a thousand miles
Serenity within this fortress sought
Our amphitheater, no one dares defile
These ivory domes encase our embalmed hearts
Within this hanging garden, we will dwell
Our luminescence shines upon the sea
We will stand tall amid colossal bells
As mausoleum columns still the breeze
Within this temple, our hearts live in sync
Upon the mountains, to our love, we drink.

## Affluence of Wonder

Burning the sage to engulf a new brand
Rich calcification is no sleight of hand
Repression and trauma, falling to the floor
Depression, dilemmas, kick them out the door

Dissolving the sorrows into the bare ground
Gushing of water declines by the pound
Tears begin running while scoping the womb
Escaping the wrath of a self imposed tomb

To separate solids, the opposites blend
To form the realities Hermes has penned
Severing egos, choose what will remain
In light of the burning and flushing of pain

Above and below, the conjunction will rise
Below and above, the bright gold is the prize
Our connections to deities rise to the top
Epiphanies crackling, revealing a pop

Fermenting and rotting, the shit hits the fan
Prima materia ceases its span
Old decomposing, breakdown persists
Let this antiquated perception desist

Distilling and purification transpires
The type of result that one often admires
Attachment to self and the heartache as well
Will mimic vibrations that send you to Hell

Coagulate, make sure the balance remains
Manifestation of riches contained
Spirit to spirit, the bridges now link
You and the world are now truly in sync.

## Prima Materia

$\mathfrak{F}$rom poet to healer
metaphor becomes medicine

From healer to muse
intention becomes inspiration

From muse to empath
whispers become winces

From empath to psychic
vexation becomes vision

From psychic to wizard
mystical becomes magical

From wizard to sage
spells become solace

From sage to artist
advice becomes aesthetics

From artist to father
paint becomes paternity

From father to Jew
gratitude becomes God

From Jew to poet
Stars become stories.

**Majesties**

Love languages, eclectic at their core
But they coincide with the universe
Our tongues operate the same more and more
Through crises, we too embrace the diverse
While we spend all our quarantine alone
This common ground we share will emanate
Decoding of the philosopher's stone
Reveals the dialect of human faith
Whether English or Spanish or Russian
Whether Chinese or Arabic or French
A poet's words will not cease in touching
Will not keep us trapped in this solemn trench
COVID-19 preys on the strong and weak
In turn, it's given us the words to speak.

**Lingua Franca**

Drunk and high upon the mountains
Remembering when pine needles
Surrounded my feet and
Injected the air with bliss

The wind comforts me
As the sun descends and
Rings the bells of a new night

I am alert in my surveillance
Under this ash tree
Which continues to stand
For ages to come

Solid as the souls I embody
Liquid as emotions invoked by ancestors
Gaseous as my dreams

I must remind myself
That I'm not alone
In this paradigm of slow animation

My walls have doors I rarely lock
And the music of warriors
Are anthems sung
To soothe the savage

Affirmed by the holy
Affirmed by the gold
Affirmed by the copper
Affirmed by the light
Affirmed by the songs
Affirmed by the lyre

My moisture is depleting
My goods and wares diminished
My prayers are solitary
My city is barren

Sought refuge in this cave
Where I control the wind
From my palms

I replenish these salty waters
The paths which lead to them
Now clearly marked

And as a wizard
I know I am good
And that the walls
To my temple
Are open

Affirmed by the holy
Affirmed by the gold
Affirmed by the copper
Affirmed by the light
Affirmed by the songs
Affirmed by the lyre

These anthems appeal to the royal
These anthems appeal to the peasant
These anthems appeal to the ancient
These anthems appeal to the embryonic

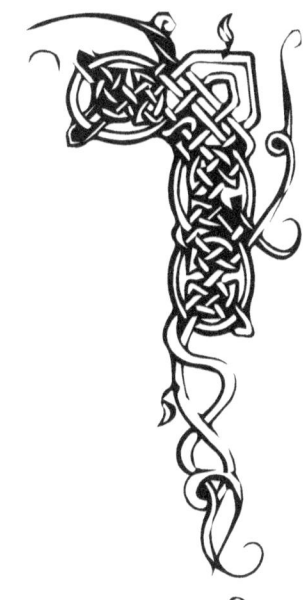

I am far from the last poet
To scribe the hymns of divinity

Even among damnation
I reserve my lips for angels

And I will not forget
Any day I left a prayer
Where the alchemy
Did not progress

Affirmed by the holy
Affirmed by the gold
Affirmed by the copper
Affirmed by the light
Affirmed by the songs
Affirmed by the lyre

This is my unofficial anthem
To a world on a morphine drip
Addicted to a construct of time
Perpetually accelerating in retrograde.

# Anthems

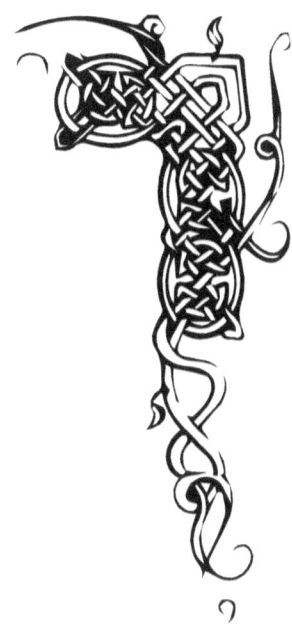

Within this confined space
Houses enmesh, privacy compromised
Longing for detachment persists
Fading memories of boundaries
Is violation in vogue?
Ecstasy – a novel concept
Wit – a quality maligned
Is fusion an abyss?
Footprints dissolve, life ferments
Beaming obscurity, conjunction coagulated

Coniunctio

Since I've written poetry
I never fit a format
Can't water down my potency
For I'm nobody's doormat

American Top 40
Will not broadcast all my lyrics
They'd cater to majorities
And censor the satiric

My trauma isn't meant to be
A trope no longer sacred
Artistically, my entropy
Is rendering me naked

Evaporating sense of self
Condensed within these verses
I just don't need this brand of help
Advice which just coerces

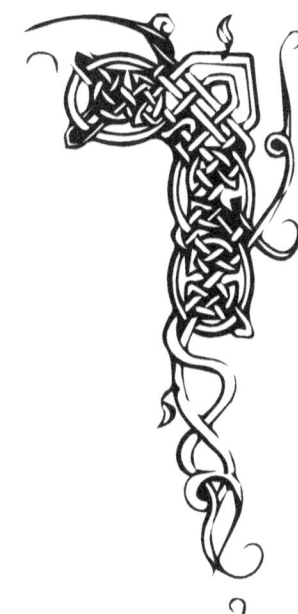

My art will not be cheapened
Cliches will not compromise
My words cannot be eaten
And for sure they are despised

I leave with you with a portrait
This fruit can't be digested
If poetry gets corporate
I will have nothing invested

For as it is these rhymes I spit
Are filled with many germs
For all normality means shit
I write on my own terms

So I'll forget the mortar board
As my words are screamed loudly
Hard knocks, electives highly scored
Now I'm Summa Cum Laude.

### Format

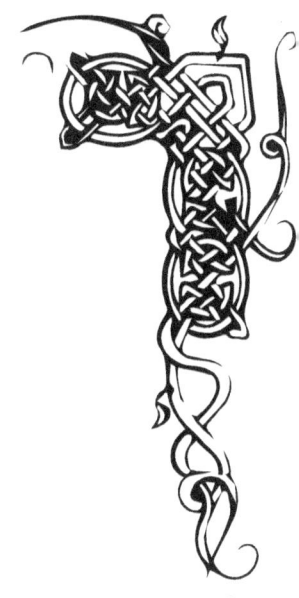

So many times, I have just walked away
Occasionally, I have forgiven
Sometimes, I take my anger day by day
Don't want to disappear for a living
My magic is meant to craft divine charms
I rarely use abilities to hex
Will not initiate magic that harms
Unless your intent is simply to vex
Virtue of patience and forgiveness last
So long as reconciliation reigns
Too hungry for companionship to fast
Too hurt for more excruciating pains
I need to place forgiveness in my heart
I need to forgive myself for my part.

## Forgiveness

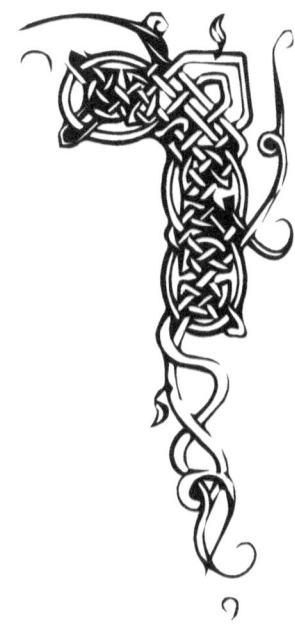

# demonology

*represents my personal demons. These are poems written to free myself of my adversity. It is important to process the darkness within in order to embrace the light.*

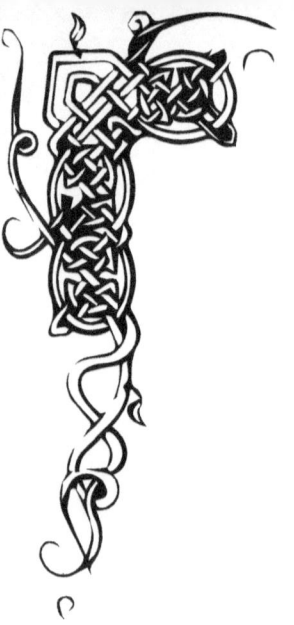

$\mathcal{L}$ast night
all my dreams
were jumbled

Woke up
in a state
of confusion

Slept again
and still...
I was unaware
of the content
of these fuzzy
remnants of vision

Could it be
a manifestation
of bipolar
mixed states?

Maybe yet
another
situation
where my
mind was
too fragile
to see clearly

I am not
engaging
well with
lack of
stimulation

Too much distance
between me and
my light

Too little space
between me and
my shadows

Imaginings
pervaded by
deficiency
of clarity

Sickness
and the fear
of fever
manifests
sadness
and paranoia

No longer
chalked up
to one
mental
health
diagnosis

To be bipolar
in a scattered world
is to be a compass

Demagnetized
and without
a clear direction
out of melancholy.

When You Can't Dream

I am alone
scared of my shadow
peering through the cracks
of a dimly lit office

Scared of my shadow
filling each corner
of a dimly lit office
which sits in the basement

Filling each corner
in my brain is a demon
which sits in the basement
succumbing to heat

In my brain is a demon
working effortlessly while I am
succumbing to heat
trapped inside these walls

Working effortlessly while I am
peering through these cracks
trapped inside these walls
I am alone.

# Pantoum: Isolation

$\mathfrak{T}$oxic positivity
Noxious infertility
Boxed invisibility
Scotch no longer filling me
Knocked into senility
Mockery is villainy
Locked within the pillory
Occidental chilling breeze
Cockamamie infancy
Rocked by tunes of infamy
Socked into infinity
Octets piss on symphonies
Chock full of these pills in me
Glock with bullets killing me
Shocked by this hostility
Crock of shit instilled in me
Octaves lacking sympathy
Rockets of duplicity
Botched all my abilities
Logic of a killing spree.

Toxic Positivity

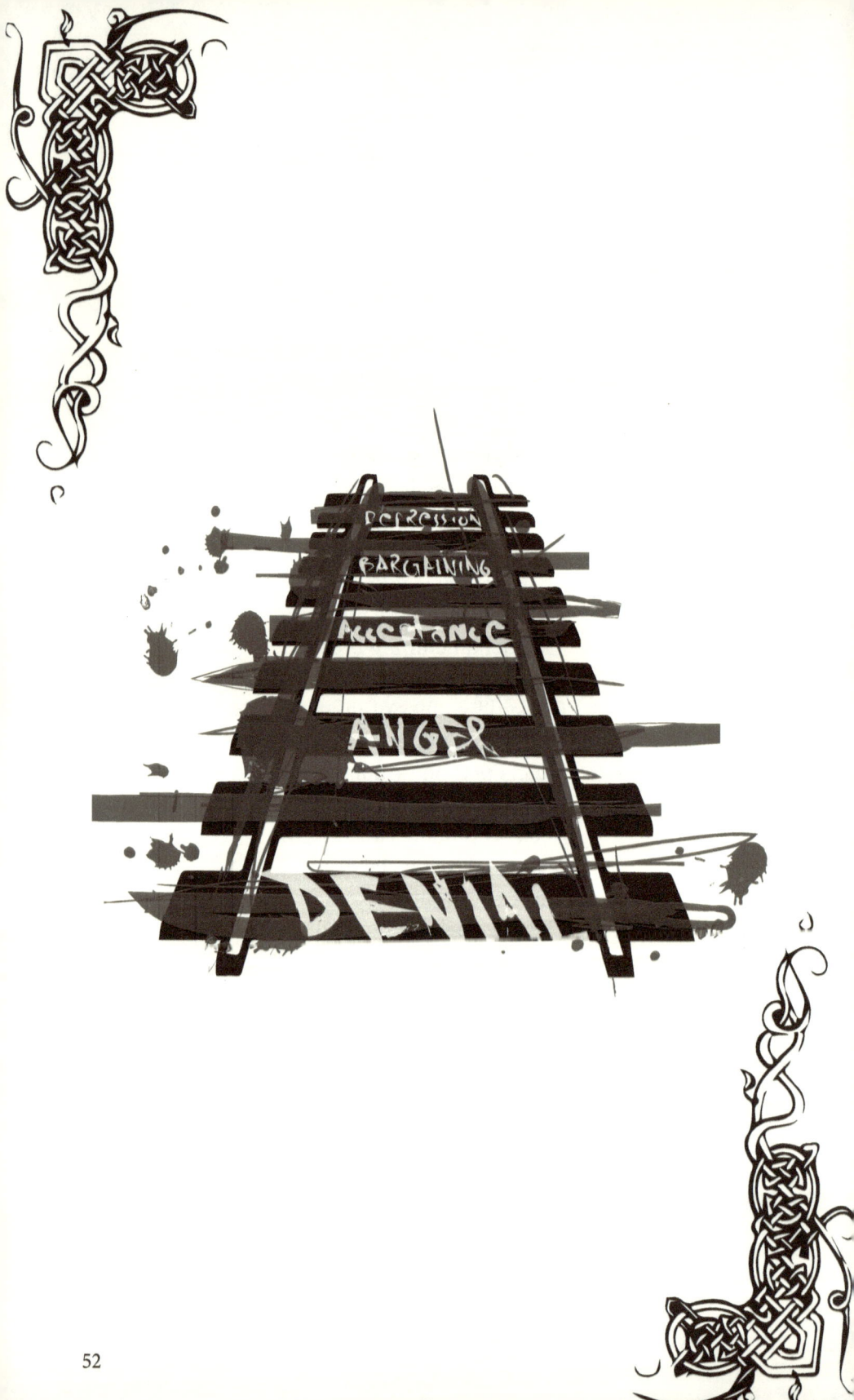

**F**unny how trains
Are attractive to the aimless

Amusing how psychosis
Enters for free
With every fare collected
From a turnstile pusher

Each stop on this train
takes the name
Of a stage in the grief cycle
It's called the Kubler-Ross Circle Line

Sometimes the track is linear
Though the timetable is inconsistent
And the order always changes
Denial
Bargaining
Anger
Depression
Acceptance

Transfers are available to the
Malebolge Express and the River Styx Ferry
Next stop is Willoughby
I got off at Willowbrook
Before leaping further
Into my hopelessness.

## 𝔐ixed 𝔖ignals

This circle underwent shrinkage
and the periphery
is protected by a force field

Can you see a clear picture
of who will stay
and who will equate
friendship with fecklessness?

Over the years
you learn that when your world crumbles
your social life crumbles with you

I can only hope
whomever inherits this earth
knows how to empathize

For the sum of all parts
is knowing the difference
between those who see you as a product
and others who admire your quotients

Intellectual and emotional alike

This inner circle is intact

It is the center of a three-ring circus
where the dead take the spotlight
as minions surround the bodies
from neighboring rings
as the coffin is lowered

Some will reach across to help

Others will simply witness your descent

But at the end of the day...
some of the cords, radii, and diameters
allow you to bounce back
keeping you suspended
as you view the full landscape
your sanctuaries span

Gestalt

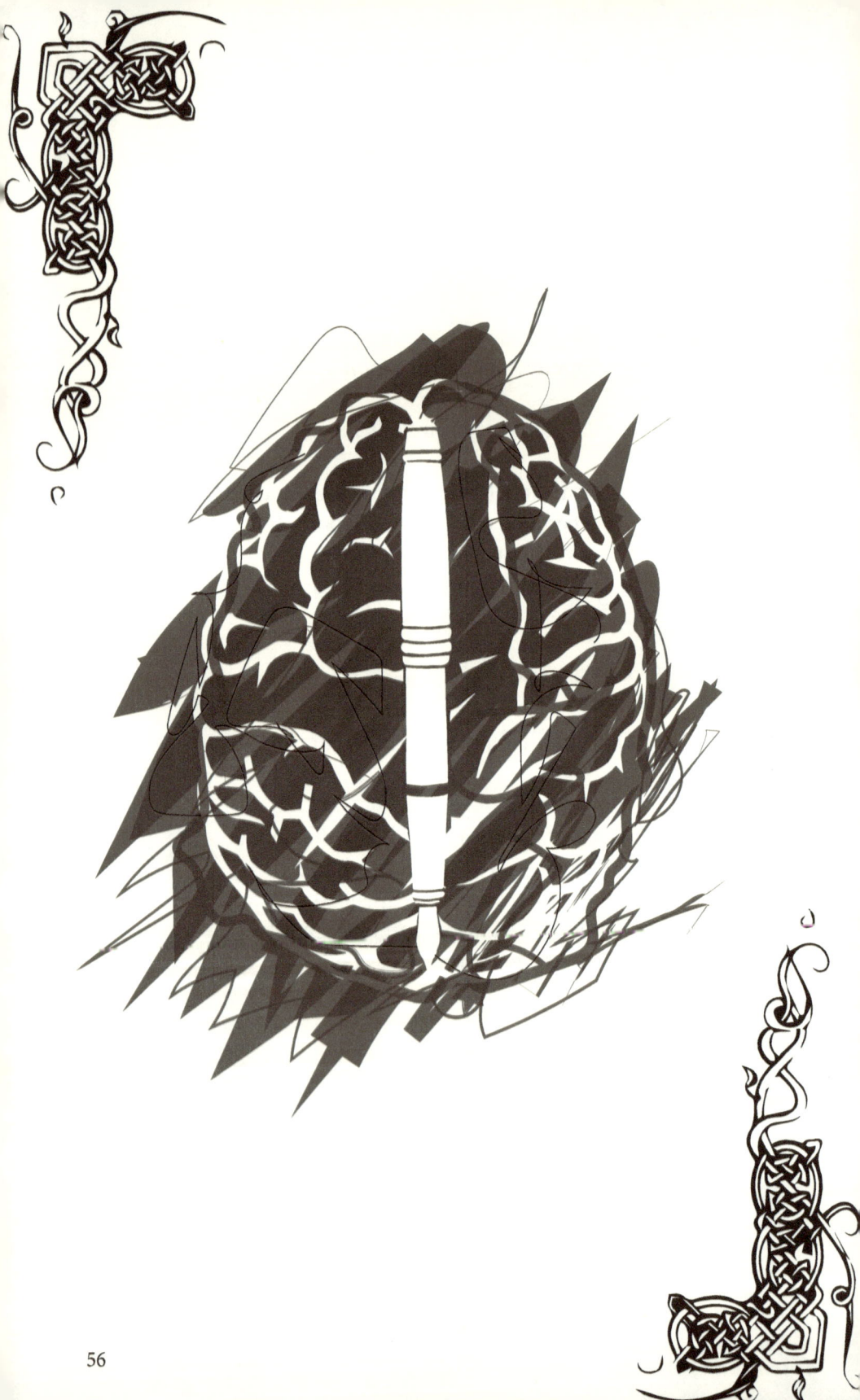

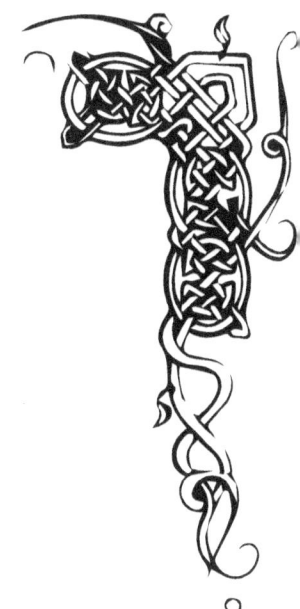

A voyeur of a decomposing mass
Spectator of a loss of vital breath
Encapsulated trauma cannot pass
When faced with the strong likelihood of death
Bore witness to a life force as it drained
A stroke of genius passing through the stem
Made breathless, atrophied, resilient brain
The blood collapsed, cell walls are now condemned
Attachments to man that could not be tamed
Have varied and relations were profound
He's eating pancakes now, for when light came
The orange and the blue flashed through his sound
From right to left, the pen switched hands and wrote
Came to the heavens, playing his last note

## Sonnet to a Stroke

Running through the middle
Attempting to survive
Even amid acquittal
This guilt remains alive

With obligations mounting
Bandwidth quickly depleting
There's way too much surrounding
Our hearts now quickly beating

Completion of the gauntlet
A race most of us ran
This is the early onset
Of mental contraband

For even after all this time
The enemies increase
In this paranoid paradigm
We all might face disease

We're just trying to live our lives
Not trying to be pithy
If one god provides us with strides
They'll look at us with pity

Now gauntlet has two meanings
A challenge and a glove
Allegiances and leanings
Won't influence above

We now have reached the summit
Convening with an owl
No intention to plummet
No throwing in the towel

Damned if clergy considers
Control to be support
Between two ancient rivers
Is where you'll find God's court.

## Gauntlet

Mastery of light
shone upon the body of
a healing soldier

Pretenses, façades
which no longer serve to mask
spiritual death

Now a corpse lies still
Passersby no longer see
his possessed body

In the heavens, he
will learn how to be in touch
with his emotions

He will keep moving
as he yearns to right the wrongs
upon this planet

In his alchemy
transformative journeys will
detoxify him

He will pass the gates
which lead to a heaven
unseen on this earth

Love will greet him there
He will know the meaning of
sharing affection

Bountiful chest of
gold transmuted through the task
of self-reflection

He will greet the world
resurrected by promise
of a clearer path

His gifts will bestow
Trees from seeds buried within
a once barren land

Now he comes back down
after stars guide him through his
resuscitation

Vision now restored
consciousness acute, now he
is alive again.

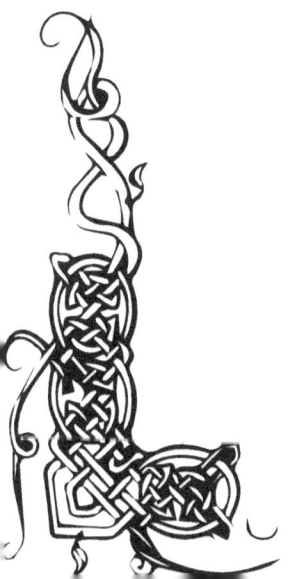

One Year Sober

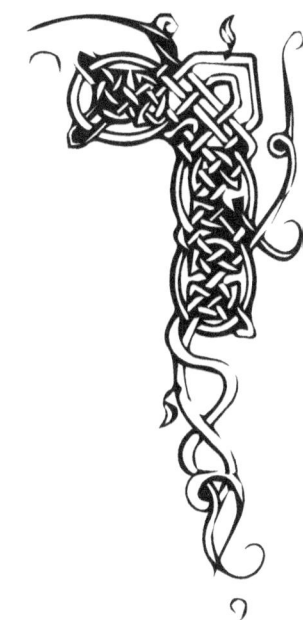

# rituals

*represents literal rituals. With my involvement in the occult,
I've made interesting discoveries through the documentation
of my rituals. This section is more of a hub of inspiration.*

In Hebrew,
the word for love
numerically corresponds
to 13.

There are 13
positive attributes of God.

Kabbalah teaches us
the transcendence of
the human ego
is represented by 13.

Death in the tarot
is attached to 13.

This represents change;
not literal decomposition.

Children become adults
when they get b'nai mitzvot
at the age of 13.

And while some fear this number
I would not be born without it.
for my grandfather was born on:

June 13, 1913.
It was a Friday!

All the positives lacking
from religious zealots
who only associate the number with evil
compose the base 13 superstitions
America possesses.

They fail to make the architecture
of our urban infrastructure
stand one story taller.

The Empire State Building
does not have a 13th floor
and those who defend this
have no ground to stand on.

## 13th Floor

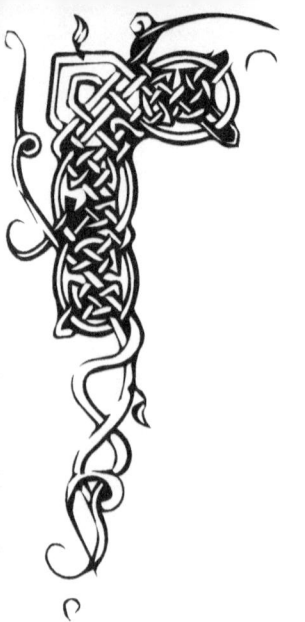

In the beginning
we learn to spell

Upon my altar
were four aces
from my tarot deck

Aces are elements
in their purest form

Medium of the spirit
directed by symbiosis

Come the witching hour
wands still commanded fire
air surrounded the sword
treasures of pentacles buried in the earth

But the water in this cup
evaporated into the atmosphere

Perhaps a reminder
that my altar
was overabundant with emotion

That my invocations
accepted my heart
as an ultimate offering

As honey jars
sealed my fortune

As thirteen pennies
supplemented the soil

As nails in a jar of urine
protected my yard

As the carcasses of mice
inside a clay planter
gave birth to
Purple Deadnettle

St. Michael watches over me
Violet rays hazy and ultra sage

Qualities which prove
pills are not needed
to witness
majesties in mountains

Grapes to Dionysus
must have fermented
in this cup

Lakshmi must have
lined it with gold

In the end
we become magick

## Missing Cup

I am trying to get though this morass
These endless days of boredom will pervade
My patience dying with melancholy
Alacrity I attempt to maintain
All the while wishing this was all a dream
Overtly dreaming and screaming aloud

This isn't happening

Especially maintaining sanity
I'm shuffling in this psychotic mess
Some still consider me the enemy
Dissenting against this autocracy
Plutocracy and oligarchy reign
Consumed by blatant demagoguery
Controlled by a megalomaniac
Wishing by some miracle of Hashem

This isn't happening

But now I'm staying somewhat productive
Attempting to write though all my anguish
Passing through life as phantoms of sickness
It's been too long since I've seen the ocean
Compassion agitated through his mess
My empathy will survive so long as

This isn't happening.

# This Isn't Happening

With every downward step
There are incremental victories
From numerical order
You embrace rapid succession

Within these three sides expanding
You reach a second dimension
Numbers successively increase
Triangular numbers form

This map of binomial expression
Every story births a new dimension
Triangles become tetrahedrons
Pyramids to the layman

Every generation of a pattern
Born from one singular source
Infinitely strong and growing
Cradled by The One.

# Ode to Pascal's Triangle

ithin the darkness
a candle beams

Can I control the flame
I sometimes struggle to control
within my belly?

I see trails of fire
pointing straight
In the divergence of the light
the orange embers
beckon me to follow
every fork in this burning highway

Every exit is a ramp
leading to peace

Fire rests upon my shoulders
when my heart and mind
converge within this meditation

My eyes are the magnet
controlling a compass
fueled by wax

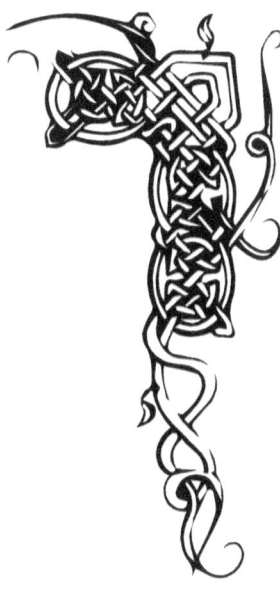

More directions exist
than I had ever fathomed

I can control the altitude
my spirit reaches
and I see heaven emanating
from a candle far from brief

I feel my sense of masculinity
forming as trails denote my chromosomes
on both the x-axis and y-axis

And even when the daylight breaks
this light won't be obscured
for the sun and the moon
within the eyes of the falcon
won't allow the night to perish

## Fire Bender

$\mathfrak{M}$y head is crested by fire
Orange jewels are my dowry from the sun
From organized follicles sprout a chaotic mane

My eyes carry water
Blue with copious traces of salt
They protect me from toxic apathy

My brain mirrors the face of the earth
Land surrounding seeds of levity
Fruit of innovation rises from greenery

My mouth releases air
Whistling hymns of passion
Fragile security blown from Bermudian sand

My jaw encases my spirit
Gold and soft-spoken
Plating my mandible with luxury.

## Anatomy of My Mask

Inside the inferno
The immolation
Of my image
Is initiated
Within a cast iron cauldron

I am burning sage
To smudge the residue
Of shadows which remain
After the lightbulbs shattered

Bay leaves raked
Over the intentions
To find the purity
I yearn to embody

Frankincense served as coals
Upon which flames
Swallowed self-pity

Meditation derived
From watching the smoke
Float from the ashes
Of the herbs

A phoenix rises
From this cauldron

Incantations follow
As my breath contains the flames
Which line
The depths
Of a void

Specters of incineration rise
Apparitions of fire dissipate

Leaving signals in smoke
Validating evanescence
And bringing
My intentions
To life.

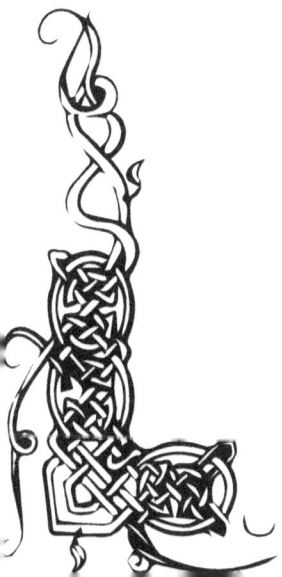

Immolate

קהילת בני יעקב

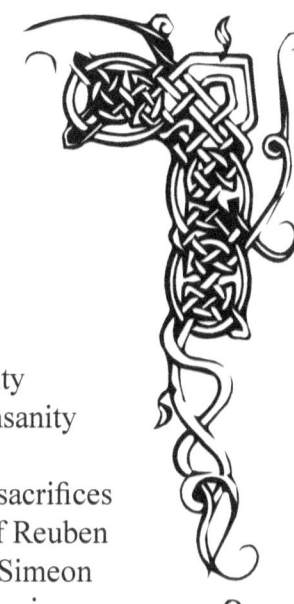

On the pink moon,
I left behind a dozen years of instability
A tribe was born for every year I tossed insanity
into the forge
Each tribe presented a gift rising from these sacrifices
My darkness illuminated by the rising sun of Reuben
My walls excavated through subterfuge of Simeon
My heart protected through vision of Levi
My weakness absolved via the lion's heart of Judah
My justice calibrated through the scales of Dan
My kindness liberated by the doe of Naphtali
My community connected with the tents of Gad
My peace harvested within the olives of Asher
My universe explored through observations of Issachar
My finances supplemented by the travels of Zebulon
My dreams realized through many prophecies of Joseph
My sacrifices rationed through the appetite of Benjamin
Indiscretions Sacrileges Lamentations Transgressions
I become the Genesis in which my evolution tells me
that Jacob is who I must be
I await the Exodus in which my revolution tells me that
Israel is who I must embody
I am the healing force who dwells in gardens inherently
nourished
I am the poet who has survived long enough to scribe
his legacy.

## Genesis of Jacob

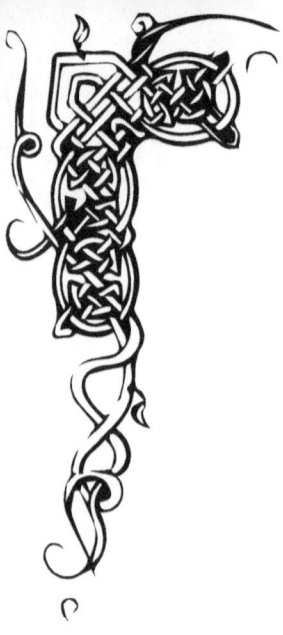

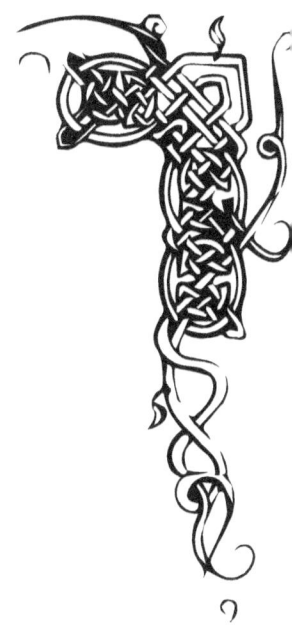

# visions

*represents the ethereal and images from the unconscious.
Dreams are great indicators for what you must know in your
waking life. The greatest discoveries come from dreams.*

My father's legacy
exists in Martling's Pond

He offered two catfish
to the soul of Clove Lakes Park

Whether they survived
is a mystery to us

But fisherman often spoke
of their presence in these waters

I remembered biology class
when I learned how fish spawn

Their offspring contained in eggs
while fertilized in their nests

One may only hope
we changed the ecosystem

Perhaps we changed this environment
with a gift reminiscent of Noah

Twenty years have passed
since we gave them up

Now their spawn eat the algae
at the bottom of the pond

Here's hoping future generations
help habitats harbor harmony.

## Vision Quest

W ithin your name, I found a legacy
Each letter spells out all our miracles
As Jews, we honor every destiny

You split the waters with a lyrical
combination of a language found
Our bricks for writing are empirical

With fire, you could see the Lord's voice bound
within a bush aiding the Israelites
It tells you how to break through this compound

A stutter never stopped you from the fight
as brother Aaron transcribed with his hand
You left an impact as Jews saw the light

From slavery and from bondage, we all ran
You were excluded for questioning God
and hence did not enter the Promised Land

We are the people who never facade
We are comforted by thy staff and rod.

### Terza Rima: Moses

Cut off the air
to overactive
reruns.

Replace them with
landscapes
within
the confines of bars

I speak not
of the kind which
house the depths of sin

I speak not
of the kind which
enable the pitfalls of vice

I speak of the test pattern
I speak of the black and the white
I speak of the red and the green and the blue

I speak of the cyan and the magenta and the yellow
They are temporary breaks
from life

They are screensavers
timed at the conveniences of networks.

Ending the day of broadcasting
Encouraging basic perception of color

These bars do not constrain.
Instead,
they narrate
the origin story
of vision

Test patterns are a reminder
of how even TV
took time to tune out

Have we lost touch with tending to our needs?

We keep going
but a temporary halt
does not disqualify us
from our hierarchy of needs

Keep
your
own
pace

Nurture
your
roots

A new day
A fresh start
Your downtime is now a spectrum.

This is Only a Test

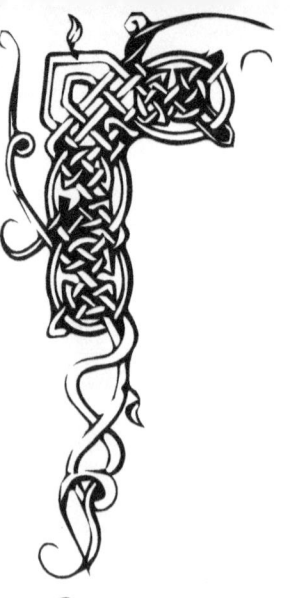

At the bottom of a hotel pool,
a lounge resides.

Three cocktails later,
you resurface toward a dome
where facets of the sun
kaleidoscopically connect.

You exit,
jump cutting to the lobby
adorned in a white fuzzy robe

To your right is a casino.
Strobe lights illuminate leagues of
gallant gamblers

Sit down and pull the handle.
Forget the buttons
and put muscle
into that desire

to press your luck.

Your results will be mixed.
There will be combinations of BAR and 7
On their individual reels.
Sometimes singular
Perhaps pairs
Theoretically, triple sets of BAR and 7 on each reel
threaten to entice you
as coins plummet like dreams after disillusionment.

You won't remember whether you came out ahead.
You won't question how you managed to carry all those coins.
You won't care how many chips you placed on your lucky number
in roulette.
You won't recall the number which brought you luck.


The croupier shouts
NO MORE BETS!
The ball settles.


You rise
as you long for the rainbow bridge
which comforted you in your bliss.


One roulette marble separates into
a plethora of pachinko balls
They ricochet through the Tokyo of your temperament.
Multi-pegged console, unpredictable mainframe.


Peter Max and Lisa Frank:
Lord and Lady of psychedelic splendor
are the ones who greet you
every time a nightmare transmutes into a dream,
paving a road reminiscent of a peacock's tail.

## Bar 7

Sueños oscuros;
Somos la única luz.
Medianoche:
La luna ya nos guía.
Entenderemos el sol.

-----

Dark dreams
We are the only light
Midnight
The moon already guides us
We will understand the sun.

## Medianoche

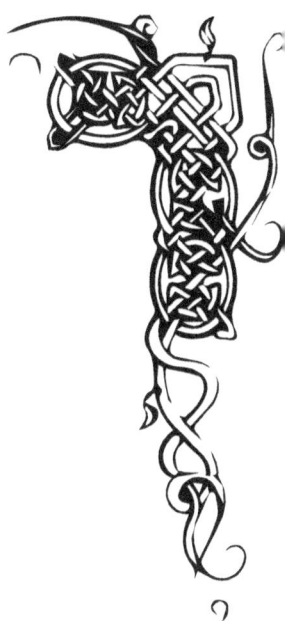

אני שר גדול
אבל אני לא השם
יש רק האחד

------

ani shar gadol
aval ani lo Hashem
yesh rak ha'Echad

------

I am a great poet
but I am not God
There is only The One.

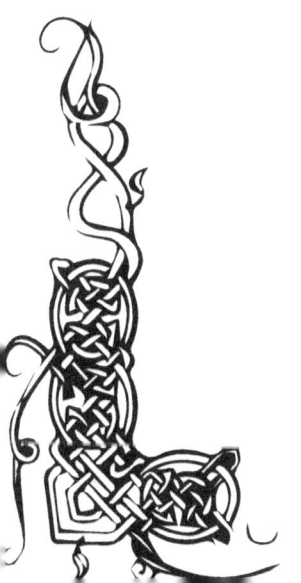

Gadol

Upon a boat
one can survey the
merging of memories
projected upon the backdrop
of a skyline marred by fear

One can
spot the wall
opening up
as it separates
into a gateway
for the healing
of broken hearts

Knowing that it's been
two decades
since we kept remembering
where we were that day
when lower Manhattan
became a metropolis of ghosts

Knowing that it's been
two decades
since we remembered
in spite of our collective trauma
beckoning us to forget

Knowing that it's been
two decades
since the monumental
loss of a monument

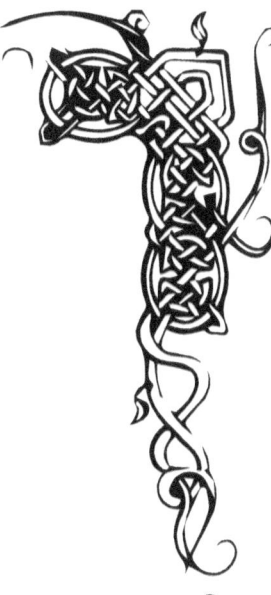

Sensations of sirens
and stenches
of sorrow
under the sunset
no longer feel
like such distant memories

This landmark
is a reminder
of how the spirit realm
formed a vortex
in which our souls
connected
within the
phantom platoon
commemorated
every September

Positioned at the helm
illuminated by two
luminescent monoliths
in place of stone

Standing stoically
as the heartbreak
of a nation
fixates upon a
landmark of light.

## Landmark of Light

Within the crystal ball,
I am rolling and weaving
orbiting within my vision is hope.

Wands crossing
Pentacles shimmering
Cups upright
Swords erect

Truth escapes from a cough
Throat chakra cleared

Energy descends to the heart.
I read the words in the reflection.
This psychic ball of glass fills with snow

Delivering this message

I AM THE HOPE
WHICH VASTLY
ENGULFS VITALITY.

Vision of Hope

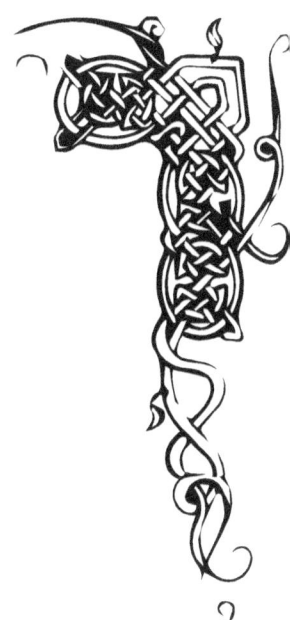

# transfiguration

*represents the impact of pop culture. Music, film, and TV are themes included in this section. These poems are dedicated to my muses.*

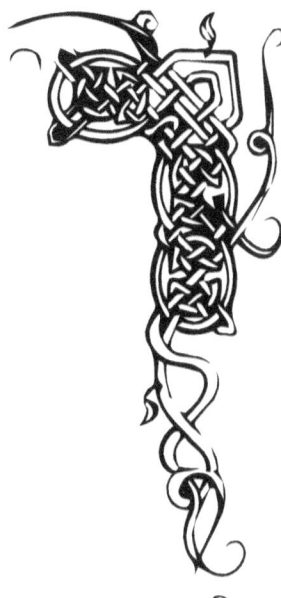

Bleakness of desert.
Cacti I have befriended.
I saw her come by
in her big red pickup truck.
Nice of her to stop and wave.

And so I wave back,
smiling as I see her pass
My eyes are wistful
filling with a deep ennui
as my whiskers hang below.

Maybe one day I
will find this companionship
and I'll be rescued
Not left in the tumbleweeds
rolling like the passing years.

Alas, I'm alone
reclining upon this rock,
hoping that Snoopy
has some leads on loving homes.
Flying Ace - take me away.

Spike

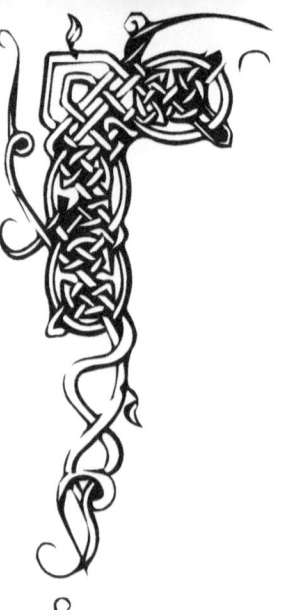

Twenty years
of the show Survivor
never prepared us for pandemics

Our fire
must always keep roaring
as we aim not to be extinguished

We're the tribe
of castaways who dare
to dream amid COVID-19 panic

Aligned are
stars and fraternity
even within lonely domiciles

The tag line:
Outwit, Outplay, Outlast
is appropriate for our struggles

Villainous
is this contagion
to which we need an immunity

The chorus
of these ancient voices
echo sentiments of starvation

Please tell me
if the tribe has spoken
to the souls of those unfit to breathe

Is it worth
one million fucking bucks
to stay stuck on this infected land?

We are not
playing a game right now
as we attempt to maintain our lives

No TV
can alleviate the
harsh terrains of our reality

Unscripted
casualties of disease
won't nullify our democracy

And now here
we are on this landscape
fearing every single element

Fishing for
a cure for all our ills
off the shore of our dystopia

Maintaining
our standing in this world
as we play this antisocial game

Torches are
standing tall as we walk
through these harsh terrains of maladies

Survivor:
forty seasons of grit
never prepared castaways for this.

Survivor

Using your voice to
speak to a generation
sometimes goes unheard
In the event someone cares
listen if the vibe suits you

Come enjoy the air
Breathing is necessary
when consuming light
from the depths of the cosmos
and the light within your soul

Running away can
only serve to cheat yourself
from felicity
Following like a stalker
are the problems you carry

Synchronicity
sometimes serves to add distress
more than oft needed
Limitations crush the mind
when constrained by Father Time

Death need not be sad
Parts of us must rot away
Consumed by living
are these insecurities
which squatted far too long

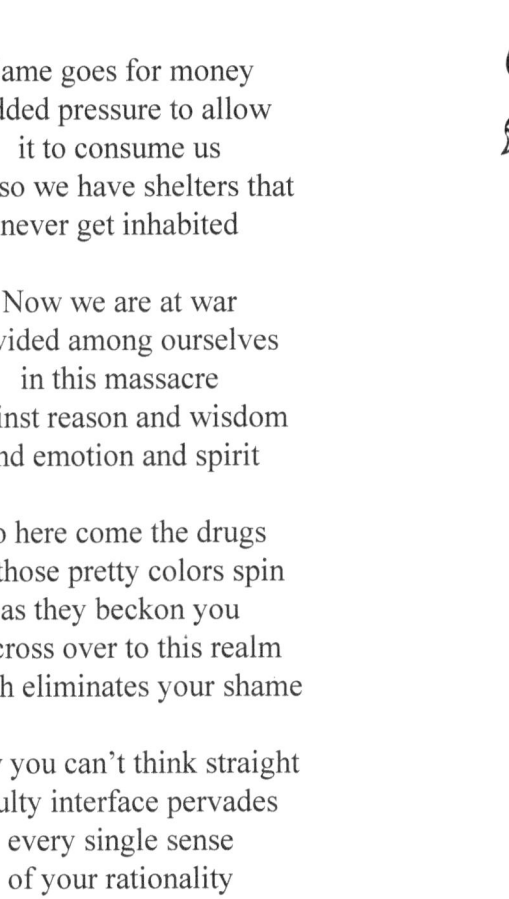

Same goes for money
Added pressure to allow
it to consume us
just so we have shelters that
never get inhabited

Now we are at war
Divided among ourselves
in this massacre
against reason and wisdom
and emotion and spirit

So here come the drugs
all those pretty colors spin
as they beckon you
to cross over to this realm
which eliminates your shame

Now you can't think straight
Faulty interface pervades
every single sense
of your rationality
falls quickly by the way side

As the world closes
memories on this journey
are fading to black
for the destination reached
is the dark side of the moon.

## Yet Another Pink Floyd Poem

Thank you for your gifts
for the city of Paris
needs your wit

Your whimsy
nourishes gardens
succumbing to
droughts and
stubborn weeds

Admittedly I forgot
what drew me to you

If I fathomed a guess
it would be that you are
the human hybrid
of a sparrow and raven

Perhaps your intuition
about the simultaneous
occurrences of
fifteen Parisian orgasms
amused my aura

You are a priestess
who can make garden gnomes
fulfill their destinies

Though you are fictional
your impact is authentic
as budding cherry blossoms
after the winter
cease to enable
reclusive habits

Kindness is always kismet
as you humbly
improve the lives around you
from inside Café des 2 Moulins

And know that when your mystique
drew love to you
through your webs of riddles
someone would crack your codes
the way you cracked your crème brûlée
and enjoyed its simplicity

All the while
your complexity
was as refreshing
as a reservoir

And I am grateful
you found that
joie de vivre.

# Love Poem to Amélie Poulain

Our cursors will keep all our ghosts at bay
Eat strife like burgers we prepare to build
Fight cosmic gangsters standing in the way
Lift fallen soldiers over war-torn hills
Driving though harsh conditions dodging guns
Aiming for flying ducks diving through screens
Pinball soaring through seas under the sun
Our futures set our psychedelic scenes
These unicycle wheels must learn to leap
Hopping upon these color changing cubes
Solar system conquest: blip, bloop, and bleep
Root beer shall flow from inside fountain tubes
Two quarters in the slot will buy your games
It's not over until you type your name.

## Colecovision

Kosher style deli
Ordered pastrami on rye
French fries on the side
Pareve egg cream satiates
While sitting on the A train
Subway car intact
Settled in the dining hall
Where I sit and nosh
To my youthful heart's content
May its memory live on.

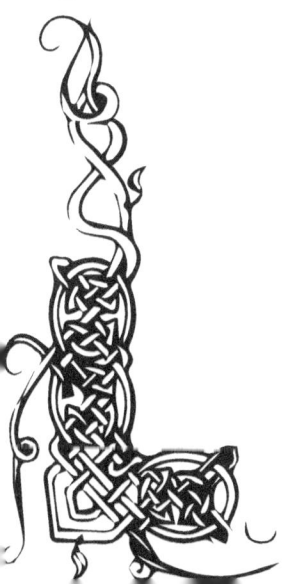

Golden's Deli

Decembers lighten
Frost embraces
Snow angels sanctify avalanches
Wings embrace embankments
Anxious eyes shout silently
Irises irrigated
Pupils positioned prominently
Blizzard breezes beckoned

Does one dare to enter the fortress?
One wailing and winding wall
After another?
Risky to touch hearts
Stone surrounding sympathy
Second skin
Blood spills from these walls
Gentle force collapses this fortress
Kindness is a tool
Chiseling defenses
Friendship flushes frustration
Laughter lavishes the landscape

Remaining open to prospects of love
Dreams lack conditions
Prophecies of better days
Emotions never die
Livelihoods merely forgotten
Repression empowers
Nihilistic norms

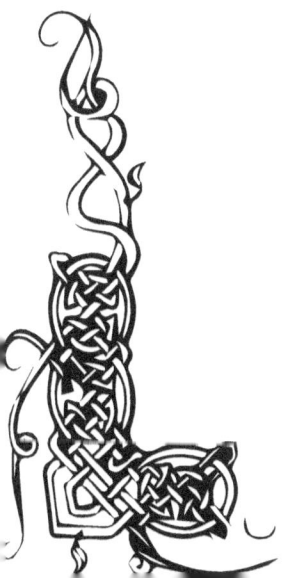

Resentment laced with poetry
Books are bricks
Building hearths meant to be shared
Never intending isolation
Poems are placenta
Nourishing knowledge

Touch of magic
Brings feeling to
Neglected nuances of nature
Rocks and islands
Empathize with
Pain and tears

I have always been a rock
I have always been an island

## Rocks + Islands

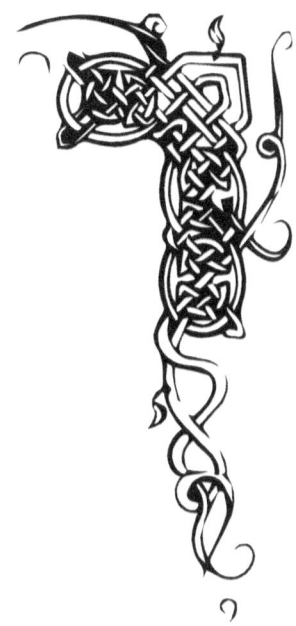

One America is the credo of brutality
Erasure of underprivileged groups called illegality
Wealthy men should file for Chapter 11 on morality
Hemming, hawing, hating – unashamed of their banality
Pushing lies in the midst of democratic mortality
Fucking up by sanctifying an alternate reality
Never knowing when they'll face career suicidality
But it's their funeral, let them tend to their own fatality.

Out of Network

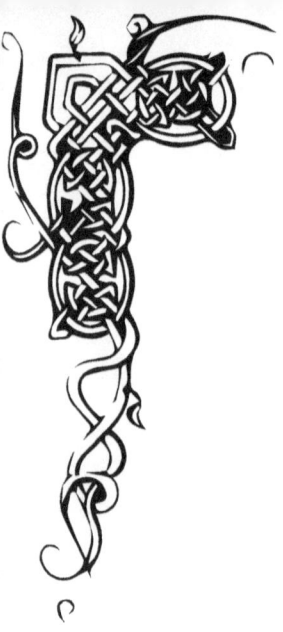

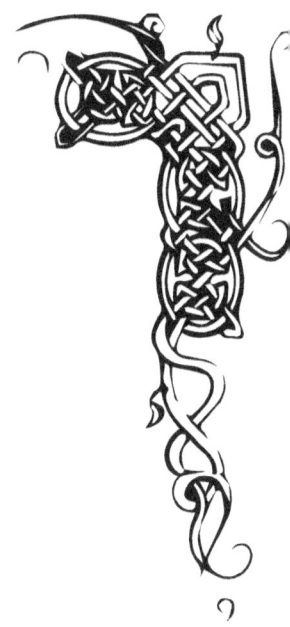

# prophecies

*represents premonitions and progress. There have been times where certain dreams became prophecies. There are always times where a brief look into the future can give you a wealth of information.*

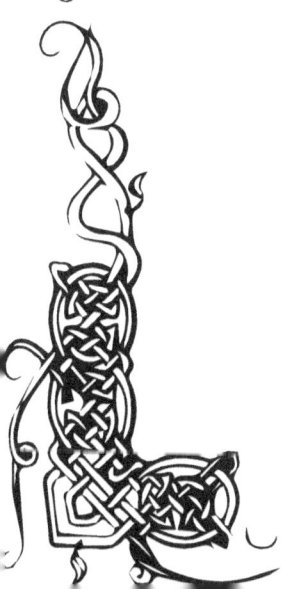

We will be the survivors of this:
Planning how to weather the storms of Armageddon

Tools at our disposal fueled by space:
That which we provide and the cosmos where we orbit

No longer do we need to assault:
In reality, our uprising is one of healing

We are already in agitation:
Protection in our hands; we are the gifts provided

In the midst of divine vision quests:
Shamanic ties between us and ancestral guidance

Periods become semicolons:
Stories still need to be told, for we are still at war

Now I find myself in this battle:
One which puts me on the front lines of viral ambush

I've got my altar to protect me:
Grapes and honey, Dionysus and Lakshmi appeased

Enriched by herbal sacraments of marijuana:
She will calm my anxiety and my depression

Masks I've worn no longer protect me:
They were the kind hiding all of my identities

My words have never been sanitized:
Though now the hands with which I write them are doused in Purell

But I'm not afraid to get dirty:
Paint and ink still are my weapons while we're struggling

Revolution is upon us now:
The kind where artists have enough time for creation

## The Revolution

I
Am
Red
Tall
Brick
Layers
Chimney
Standing
Exhausted
Monolithic
Resurrected
Renaissances.

# Chimney

Could I just open
Myself to understanding
From a gentle soul?
Nexus forming between us?
Synergy and syzygy?

Is there a connect?
Six eyes linked with visuals?
Whether in plain sight
Or in psychic energies
Bridging eccentricities?

Please solve these riddles
Without force and impatience
Be meticulous
Show me you put in effort
Without rushing this process

No doubt, you can win
Answer questions correctly
Faithful safe cracker
You don't have confirmation
Without my combination.

## Unsolved Syzygy

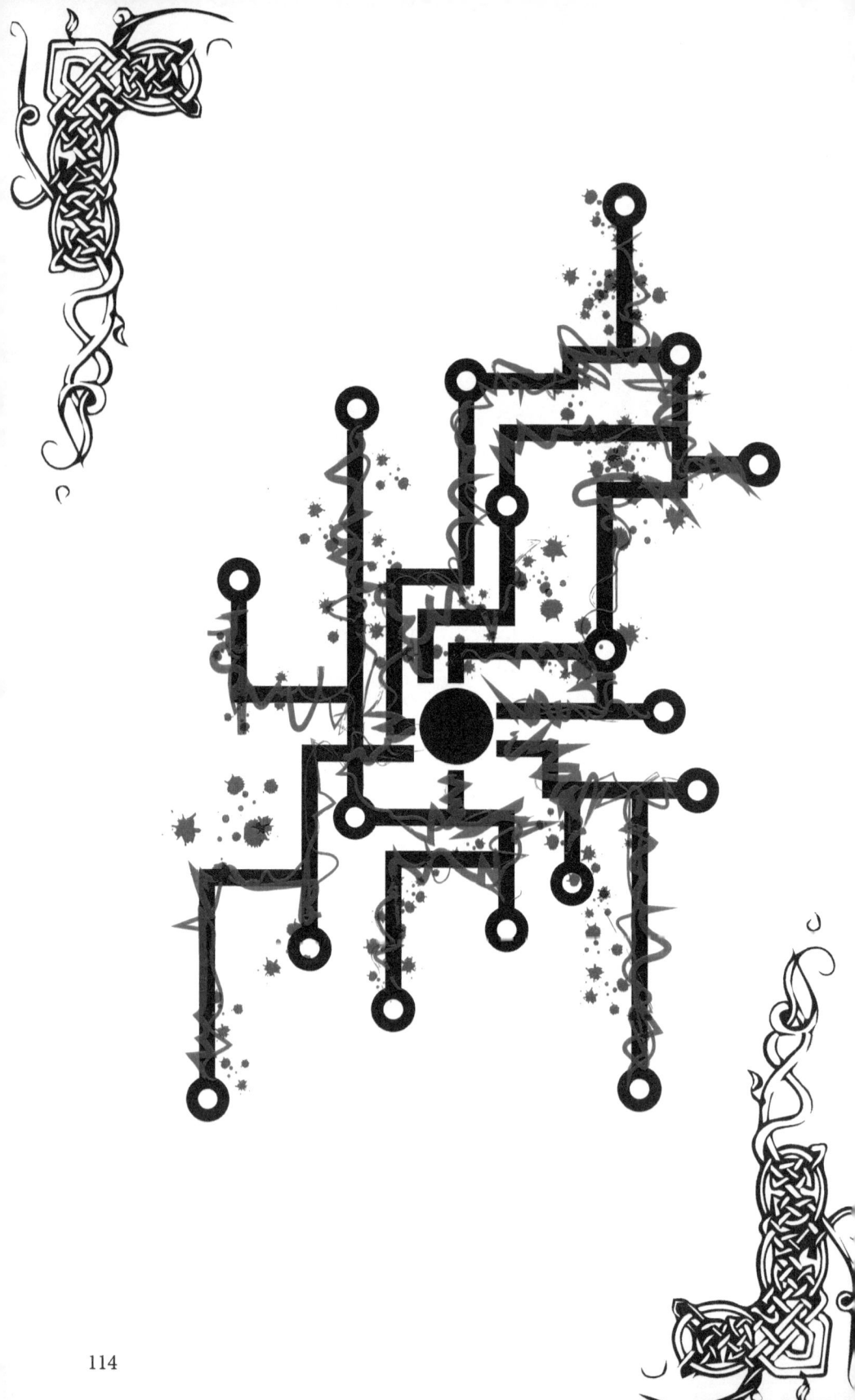

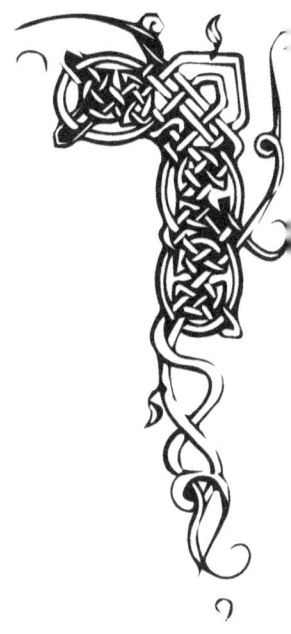

Every time I wake from
Slumber, I am more easily
Startled during morning, noon, and
Evening hours; terror purveyed by
Networks and cables and satellites
Televising this necessary foray into
Introversion; which I no longer
Attribute to shyness, but the
Loneliness thrust upon the masses.

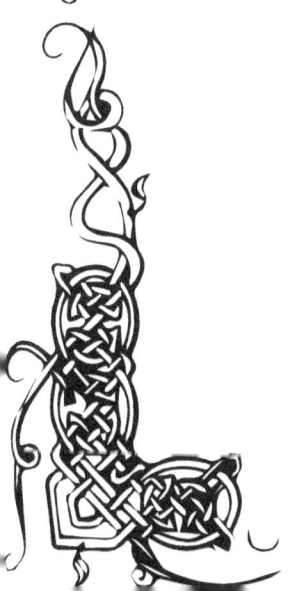

Essential

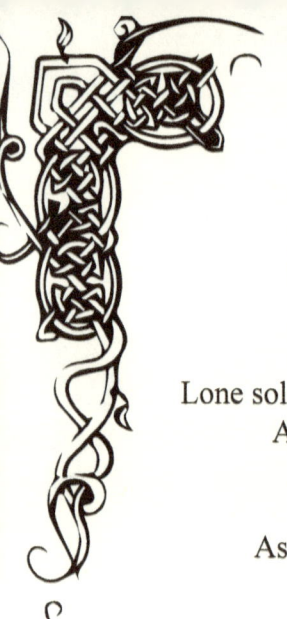

Ennui on display in this diorama
Prisoner of psychological warfare

Lone soldier in fatigues in the corner of a padded cell
Arms held in bondage by a straitjacket

Backdrop sometimes changes
As he visualizes the orange trees of Israel
From the back channels
Of his keenly focused third eye

He will think about the days he welcomed dirt
Days when trenches were used to plant trees
Rather than hiding in fear

His child will be present
Images of his fatherhood
Stay in the forefront

This soldier's lap
Will hold space
For the son he loves
And the apparitions of innocence
He wishes to contact

Even amid his lack of control
He will continue to grow

He will accept embraces
Even if he can't return them

This soldier is held in high regard
For the ways in which he survived

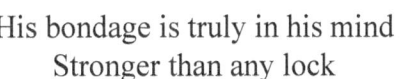

His bondage is truly in his mind
Stronger than any lock

Within this spotless window
He can see the future

No longer a soldier in combat
Always honored for his service
Even when said service
Could have killed him

This diorama is a collection
Of all the beauty he will receive
After he gave his body to a war

His heart will be a present
To all who see his love
And the key releasing his arms
Is his ability to receive
And just one exposure to affection
Will set them free

He will embrace the good
It will be seen and heard

Freedom will be on the horizon
Beyond the invisible wall
Of a diorama.

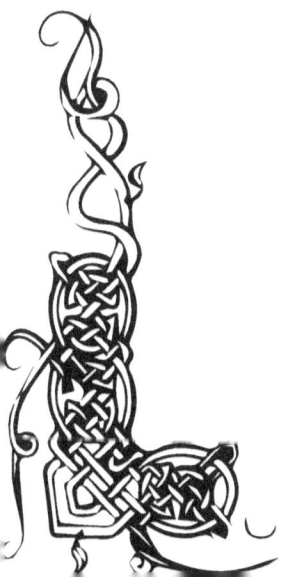

Diorama

Embrace our common ground, love, as we lay
Under the branches of a willow tree
Evolving, knowing what will be will be
Only these instincts are what we obey
My heart alone, it needs a harbinger
One who can love me when I'm my worst fiend
Within our glance, I hope this time won't end
We whisper as we hold each other near
Ignore these forces, those which interdict
We seek refuge, a tent formed by each wing
Though we're the monarchs, we will not be strict
We know in the end, we'll marry a king
Your head on my chest as I stroke your hair
We will collectively maintain our lair.

## Kings of the Castle

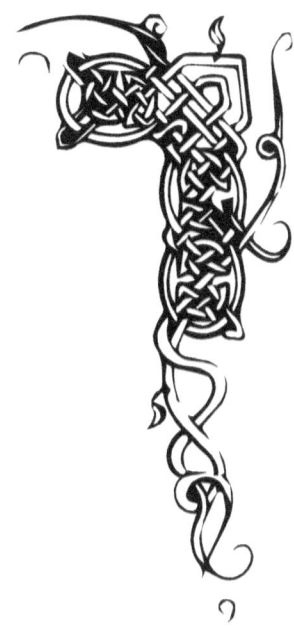

$\mathfrak{M}$oonshine
sipped in secret
potency bountiful
within the wood of the willow
burning
sunshine
walking on water, grass, and snow
glimmering compassion
blessings of love
in stars.

Celestial Mirror

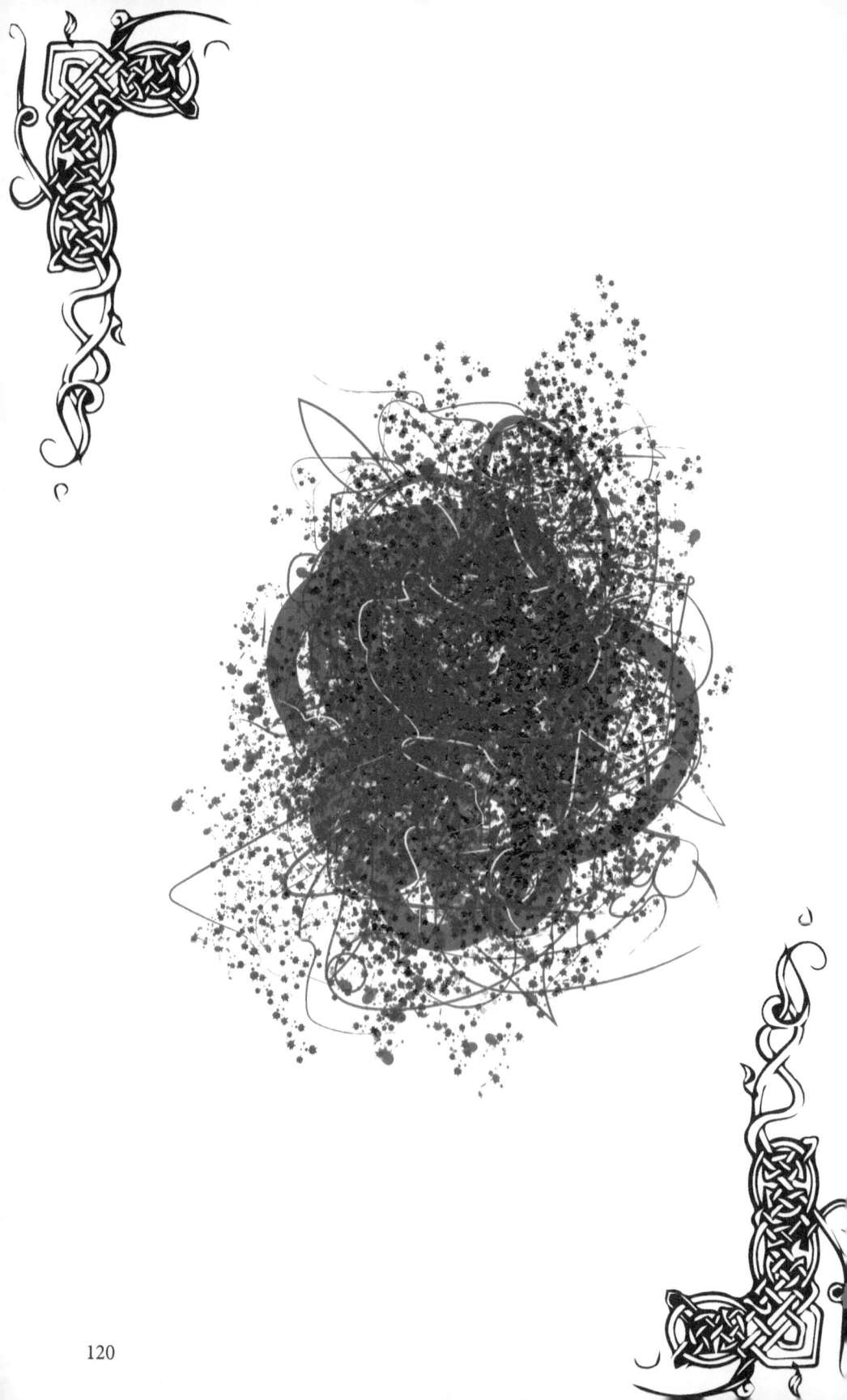

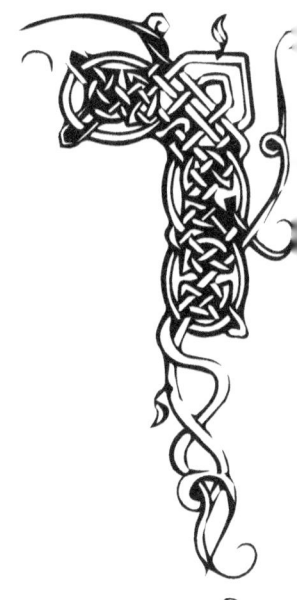

My greying process exists in the soul
As well as in my magick and my beard
And whether I will welcome getting old
My age will not be something that I fear
In my journey for wisdom, I've declared
My nonconformity as impetus
So once again, aging won't get me scared
I'm done with acts which are promiscuous
Aroma of rosemary and orange
Both scents which fill the air with strong flavors
I've bathed; I've smoked; I've burned; and I've foraged
Help my greying magick without sabres
Ridiculous and certainly sublime
My hair will lose color when it is time.

## Greying

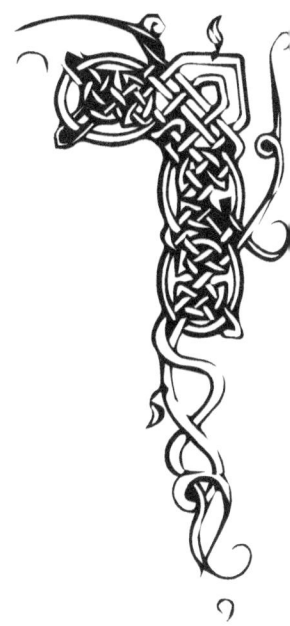

# Manifestations

In January, may we, as a universe, realize our potentials for greatness and serve as a beacon of light.

In February, may we no longer struggle to survive in a society which stacks the odds against the needy.

In March, may we realize that we must strive for peace in a paradigm of war.

In April, may we mourn the loss of perception and heal from the lies we once embraced.

In May, may we trust that the universe has plans for our collective healing.

In June, may we expand our visions to that which lies beyond this physical realm.

In July, may we abandon our addictions to information and adopt critical thought to shape our view of the world.

In August, may we no longer demonize that which we do not understand.

In September, may we truly embrace our successes and the successes of our fellow citizens of Earth.

In October, may we welcome the light within ourselves and share it with those struggling with darkness.

In November, may we allow love to flourish as we abandon the perils of resentment.

In December, may we stand up for ourselves and assert our rights to exist.

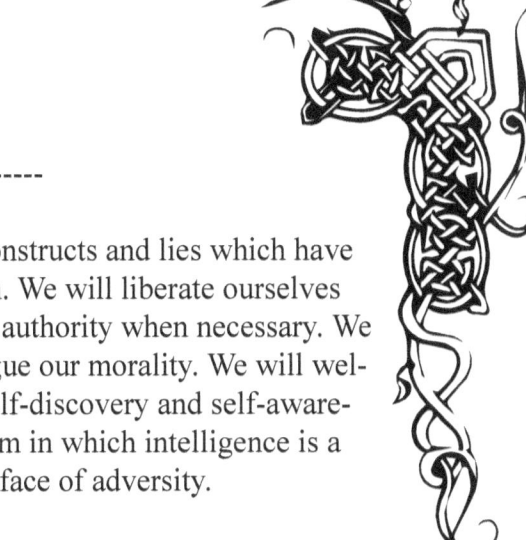

------

We will exile the social constructs and lies which have damaged our compassion. We will liberate ourselves from delusion and question authority when necessary. We will not allow greed to plague our morality. We will welcome the beginnings of self-discovery and self-awareness. We will enter a realm in which intelligence is a strength in the face of adversity.

Banish the compulsion to blindly obey even amid our instincts saying the opposite. Banish the perception that financial wealth is the only form of abundance which matters. Banish the need to abandon ourselves to serve another master.

Every journey begins with emotional tummult and ends with an evolved soul.

Isis-Astarte-Diana-Hecate-Demeter-Kali-Inanna
Isis-Astarte-Diana-Hecate-Demeter-Kali-Inanna
Isis-Astarte-Diana-Hecate-Demeter-Kali-Inanna

So mote it be. So mote it be. So mote it be.

------

# the author

# Jacob R. Moses
## (AKA Jack M. Freedman)

is a poet and spoken word artist from Staten Island, New York. Publications featuring his work span the globe. Countries in which poems found homes include USA, Canada, UK, Ireland, France, The Netherlands, Ukraine, Nigeria, South Africa, Mauritius, Pakistan, India, Bangladesh, Singapore, and Thailand. This collection of poems is an omnibus of works collected from his previous chapbooks: ...and the willow smiled (Cyberwit, 2019), Art Therapy 101 (Cyberwit, 2019), and Seance (Cyberwit, 2020). He is currently a student at Southern New Hampshire University (SNHU) pursuing an MA in English and Creative Writing with a concentration in Poetry.